Michael Scott is an authority on the
folklore of the Celts and has written over
eighty books, including the bestselling
Irish Folk and Fairy Tales. Michael Scott lives
in County Dublin.

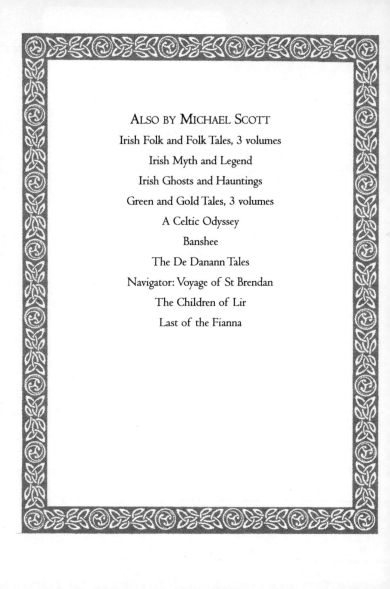

THE BOOK OF
CELTIC
WISDOM

MICHAEL SCOTT

LIR

Hodder & Stoughton

CONTENTS

Acknowledgements

Rarely can an author identify when and where an idea for a book first gestated. This book is the exception.

The author gratefully acknowledges the inspiration of Ruth Shern and Breda Purdue, the enthusiasm of Sheila Crowley and the assistance of Angela Herlihy.

The author should also like to thank Liam MacUistin for permission to quote 'Rinneadh Aisling Dúinn – We Saw a Vision'.

INTRODUCTION

No single book can encompass the wisdom of the Celts. This was a race which loved language, which held the Bard and the Poet to be the equals of Kings, indeed a race where the rulers went in fear of being satirised by a Poet — which was considered the ultimate disgrace. This was also a race without a written language, where the teachings were committed to memory and passed down in an oral tradition which is still very much alive today.

Caesar suggests in *De Bello Gallico* that

the Celtic Druids and Bards trained for twenty years, though the truth is probably far closer to twelve years. In that time, each scholar was expected to learn nearly 600 full-length stories, more than 250 poems, and also the complex laws, philosophies, grammar, history, legends and genealogies of the tribes and clans, as well as the art of divination, seership and composition. For not only were the bards expected to preserve the knowledge of the past, they were confidently expected to add to that body of knowledge.

The role of Druid and Bard, priest and scholar, cleric and storyteller was often indistinguishable, and time has blurred the lines ever further, with the result that the lore which has survived to this day is often a mixture of the sacred and the profane, the spiritual and the commonplace. This was a living lore, used in everyday life, much of it concerned with the land and the lives of the ordinary people, and it remains relevant to this day.

The following selection of Celtic wisdom, gathered from numerous sources, seeks to reflect the body of knowledge which a Bard would most likely have possessed; it is a mixture of folktales and legends, poems and proverbs, triads and blessings. Use them well.

And always follow the older Bard's injunction to the young student: Speak slowly, think swiftly, act wisely.

THE SONG OF AMERGIN

Amergin White Knee, the ancient teacher who accompanied Eber Donn the Milesian leader to Ireland, is credited with the composition of this great paean to the elemental forces, 'the spirit man calls God'. In one version of the tale, he recites the poem as he steps ashore on the ancient land, but in another, even older version of the tale, he is merely the vessel through which the tripartite goddess of Ireland,

Banba, Fodla and Eriu greet the latest invaders to their shores. Powerful and haunting, it reminds us that we can achieve anything we set our mind to, that there are no limits.

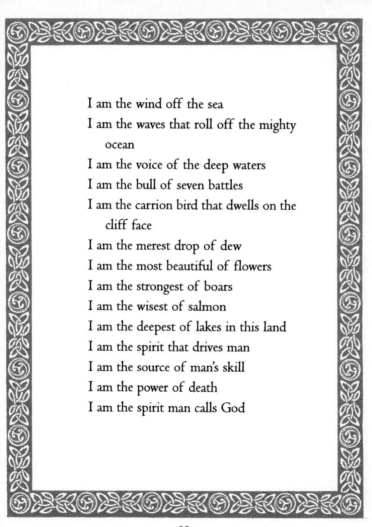

I am the wind off the sea
I am the waves that roll off the mighty
    ocean
I am the voice of the deep waters
I am the bull of seven battles
I am the carrion bird that dwells on the
    cliff face
I am the merest drop of dew
I am the most beautiful of flowers
I am the strongest of boars
I am the wisest of salmon
I am the deepest of lakes in this land
I am the spirit that drives man
I am the source of man's skill
I am the power of death
I am the spirit man calls God

TRIADS

The number three and groupings of three occur everywhere in the Celtic world – the earliest invaders were greeted by the tripartite goddess, Banba, Fodla and Eriu – and the triskele, the three-horned circle, is a common ornamental device. In Irish mythology, the most famous goddess, the Morrigan, the goddess of War, is also part of a trio, along with her sisters, Babd the Crow and Nemain, whose name signifies panic. Perhaps this tripartite nature is meant to signify the phases of the moon: full, waxing and waning. Robert Graves suggests that it might be equated with Maiden, Matron and Crone, or Virginity, Fertility and Death.

There are Three Sorrows of Irish storytelling, classic tales of doomed love and redemption: the Children of Lir are sentenced to thrice 300 years' enchantment in the form of swans, there are three Sons of Tuireann, the Celtic version of the Quest of Jason and the Argonauts, and Deirdre, the tragic heroine of the greatest of the Sorrows, flees with her lover Naoise and his two brothers.

Diogenes tells us that the Druids taught their mysteries in groupings of three.

Hilary, the Bishop of Poitiers, AD 350, and author of *De Trinitate*, was principally responsible for the concept of the Trinity in the Christian tradition, which is at the heart of the Christian faith. Even the tribal system of the Celtic lands was tripartite: priests, warriors and farmers, each one inextricably interlinked with the other.

It should be no surprise that the concept of triads entered Irish lore. The perfect triad, a single idea with three suggested answers, is central to many of the proverbs and lore of the Celts. And they are all timeless.

These are the three rudest things one can see in this world:

A youngster mocking an old man,
A hale person mocking an invalid, and
A wise man mocking a fool.

❦

There are three things that make a fool wise:

Learning,
Application, and
Patience.

And there are three things that make a wise
man foolish:
 Quarrelling,
 Rage, and
 Drunkenness.

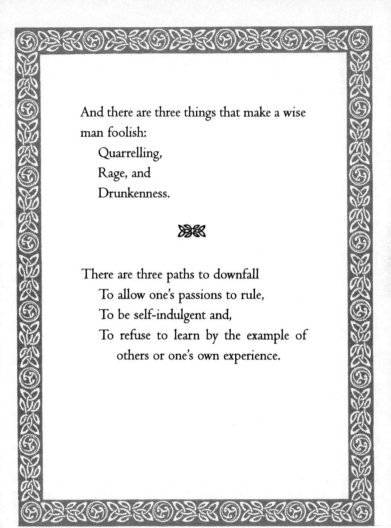

There are three paths to downfall
 To allow one's passions to rule,
 To be self-indulgent and,
 To refuse to learn by the example of
 others or one's own experience.

There are three roads to greatness
    To be wise in word
    To be wise in deed, and
    To be wise enough to control one's own
        passions.

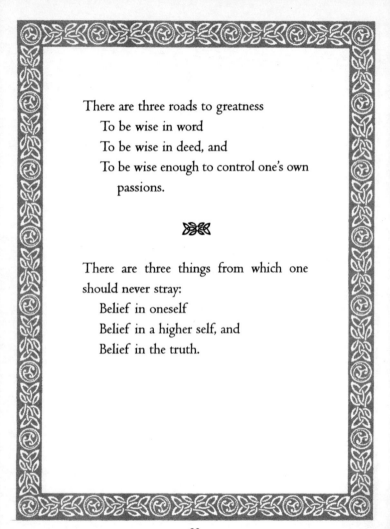

There are three things from which one should never stray:
    Belief in oneself
    Belief in a higher self, and
    Belief in the truth.

There are three things that one should never approach,
    A liar,
    A thief and,
    A knave.

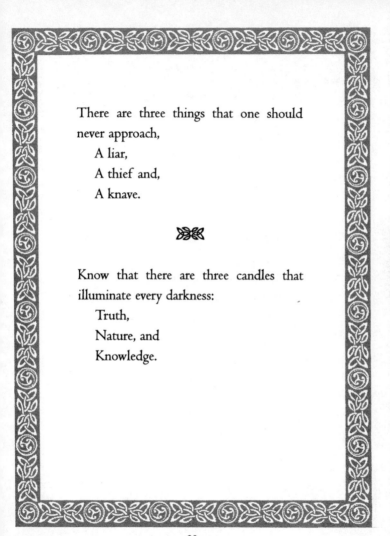

Know that there are three candles that illuminate every darkness:
    Truth,
    Nature, and
    Knowledge.

Judgement demands these three:
    Wisdom,
    Consideration, and
    Expertise.

Judgement can be determined only if these
three are present:
    Evidence which tells a tale
    Witnesses who tell the truth and
    The wisdom to evaluate both.

The three demands of Justice are
    Judgement,
    Appraisal, and
    Conscience.

⚜

Success stems from action and there are
three ways to act:
    By thought,
    By word, and
    By deed.

⚜

The three habits that lead to success:
    Patience,
    Application, and
    Vision.

The three habits that lead to failure:
    Laziness,
    Distraction, and
    Daydreaming.

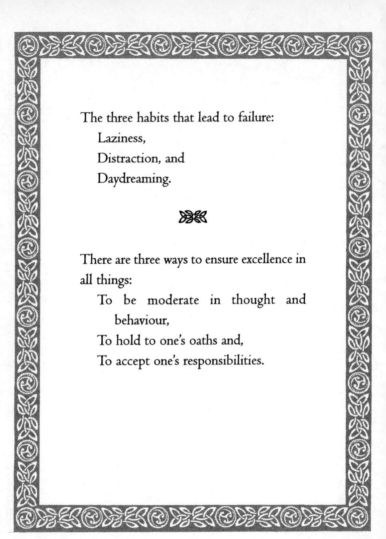

There are three ways to ensure excellence in all things:
    To be moderate in thought and behaviour,
    To hold to one's oaths and,
    To accept one's responsibilities.

One should strive to emulate these three traits in others:

Wisdom in words and deeds,

Justice in words and deeds,

Generosity in words and deeds.

There are three wonderful things in this world:

To forgive a wrong,

To make amends, and

To dispense only justice.

New life and new beginnings come from
three things:
>   The rounded belly of a woman,
>   The white smoothness of an egg, and
>   A wrong that has been forgiven.

There are three things that are better than
riches:
>   Health,
>   Freedom, and
>   Honour.

There are three needs which carry no shame:
Love,
Thirst, and
Happiness.

There are three ways to love:
With the heart,
With the mind,
With the soul.

There are three sacred qualities of love:
To save,
To shield,
To surround.

❧

Be patient and achieve this trinity of blessings:
Love,
Tranquillity, and
Contentment.

Be careful and these three will be yours:
    Respect,
    Abundance, and
    Contentment.

� decorative ornament✢

Be always timid and you will achieve,
    Nothing good
    Nothing bad
    Nothing.

✢

At the heart of every friendship, one will
find these three:
    Respect.
    Trust and
    Understanding.

This is the badge of the Fianna, and should be the badge of all men:

    Let us always have truth in our hearts,
    Let us always strive for strength in our hands,
    Let us always ensure consistency in our tongues.

The three greatest gifts of music and song:

    The pleasure it brings the assembly,
    The pleasure it gives the listener,
    The pleasure it brings to the maker.

To understand a person, one must observe them
  Awake,
  Asleep, and
  In action.

❧

These are the three sharpest things in the world:
  A thorn in the soft part of the foot,
  The burn of a rope on the palm of the hand, and
  The word of a fool.

Pride can strip us of these three things:
Time,
Money, and
Conscience

✖

There are three things that prey upon the weakest:
An enemy always attacks the weak,
The weak are vulnerable to the lure of money, and
Those who suffer the sin of pride are weak.

It is impossible to fully recompense
    A good parent,
    A patient teacher, and
    A loving partner.

※

The innermost thoughts of a person can
be unlocked by
    Love,
    Trust, and
    Drunkenness.

※

There are three things which all men seek
more of:
    Long life,
    Unfailing good health, and
    Abundant wealth.

There are three things which all men seek less of:
Sickness,
Poverty, and
Loneliness.

❧

All diseases and illness may ultimately be conquered by these three:
Patience – to endure the illness,
Time – for all things come to an end, and
The nature of the illness itself, for some have an allotted span of time and will ultimately run their course.

At the heart of every injustice there are three:
    Lies,
    Rage, and
    Greed.

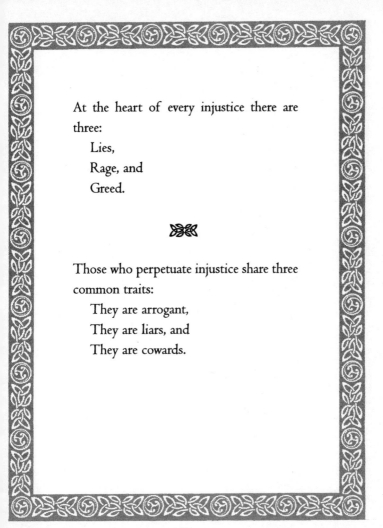

Those who perpetuate injustice share three common traits:
    They are arrogant,
    They are liars, and
    They are cowards.

Three aspirations of the honest man:
> To be honest in one's dealings with others,
>
> To be honest in one's dealings with one's partner, and
>
> To be honest in one's dealings with oneself.

�֍

Three further aspirations of the honest man:
> To conduct oneself with dignity and pride,
>
> To conduct one's business with dignity and pride, and
>
> To conclude one's business with oneself and others with dignity and pride.

For those of ill temper who learn to control that emotion, there are three immediate results:

The respect of others

The strength of character, and

The consolation of the temperate.

❋

There are three people one should never do business with:

The person too eager,

The person too greedy, and

The person too desperate.

The three signs by which you will know
the excellent physician:

    That he may examine you painlessly,

    That he may cure you completely, and

    That he may leave neither scar nor
        bruise behind.

Society is founded on these three:

    The nature of peace,

    The nature of justice, and

    Natural order.

PROVERBS AND SAYINGS

D istinct from the triads of the Gaels
are the proverbs and sayings. The
majority of these, in one variant or
another, would be common to all the
Celtic lands, while others would appear in
almost identical wording in Irish, Scots
Gaelic, Welsh and Manx, showing either
the very close cross-pollination of the
cultures or the essential truth of the
statements.

Proverbs are single ideas, slices of history, wry observations on life or perhaps bitterly learned experiences that have been honed through the ages until they can, in a single succinct sentence, express a profound truth.

There is no lack in this life like the lack of a true friend.

❦

Better a good enemy than a bad friend.

❦

A true friend and a bitter enemy both believe that you are immortal. Live as if you are trying to prove them both correct.

❦

It is far better to be alone than in bad company.

A friend that can be bought is not worth buying.

※

To be a friend to others, one must first be a friend to oneself. But to be a friend to oneself, one has to know oneself.

※

An abiding friendship is forged in hardship. An abiding friendship will survive hardship.

※

A true friend will sit alongside you – and not in your place.

A friend's eye is a good mirror. We should try and see ourselves through the eyes of our friends.

⁂

Take care: the person that will tell others' faults to you – will tell yours to others.

⁂

Waste not your time with gossips, liars and fools, lest you too will become a gossip, a liar and a fool.

⁂

Come slowly to friendship and before you make a friend, break bread together more than once.

Two see more than one, but three see less than two.

❧

Better to bend than to break. Better to break than to crumble.

❧

Lessons learned in hardship will endure; lessons lightly learned are soon forgotten.

❧

Your son is your son until the day he marries, but your daughter is your daughter until the day you die.

A mother takes the side of her son, while the father sides with the daughter. This is how is has been through the ages; this will not change.

✻

It is the lot of parents to hold their children's hands for just a brief spell, and carry them for an even shorter spell. But they carry them in their heart forever.

✻

Praise the child and you praise the mother.

Youth sheds many a skin as it grows. Experience comes through growth, and neither growth nor experience is without tribulation. This is the price of growth.

❧❧❧

Sense does not come before age. There is many a wise youth and an equal number of old fools.

❧❧❧

Even the wise man can make mistakes. The wise man will make his mistake only once while the fool insists on repeating his mistakes.

It is always better to be underestimated.

❧

Show your teeth only when you intend to bite. Never make an idle threat. And never threaten if you are not prepared to carry out the threat.

❧

Let the children do their own growing, do not shape them into a semblance of the parent.

If we are without knowledge of our past, then we are without knowledge of ourselves.

❊❊❊

Youth has no care where it sets its foot – but make sure the foot is well shod.

❊❊❊

The old cock crows and the young cock learns.

❊❊❊

The old broom best knows the dirty corners.

The older the fiddle, the sweeter the tune.

❁

The wild goose never raised a tame gosling.
The wild hound never reared a tame pup.

❁

There is no secret that is known by three.

❁

The safest secret is known only by one.

❁

There is no bone in the tongue, and yet the
same did often break a man's head or cut
his throat for him.

The tongue is the sharpest weapon of all.

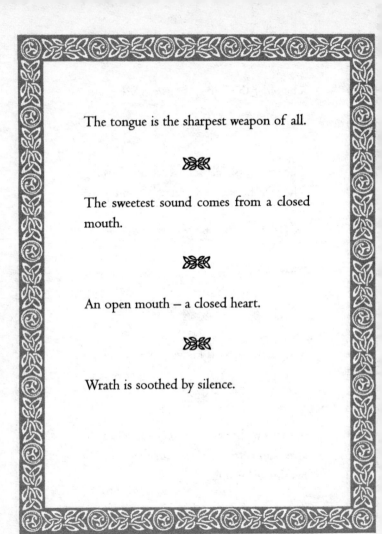

The sweetest sound comes from a closed mouth.

An open mouth – a closed heart.

Wrath is soothed by silence.

Little said is well said.

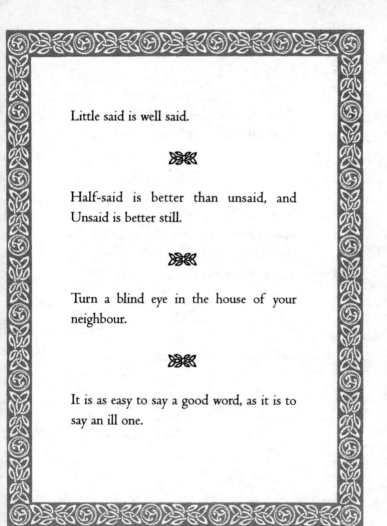

Half-said is better than unsaid, and Unsaid is better still.

Turn a blind eye in the house of your neighbour.

It is as easy to say a good word, as it is to say an ill one.

Better you say what you are afraid to hear than some say it for you.

※※※

There is some protection from one's enemy, but none from the liar. Only an upright reputation and solid friends are proof against lies and half-truths.

※※※

Great talk oft leads to little action.

※※※

Treachery always returns to its source.

Words have a magical power. They can raise up the spirits or dash them down. They can bring laughter as easily as tears. Spend words like a miser counting coins. Make each word count.

✥

It is better to consider what you will be than what you are now or what you have been. Look to the future and remember that it comes soon enough.

✥

Everything has a price. Be prepared to pay that price. But be aware that some prices are not worth paying.

What is near to the heart is always near to the mouth.

❧

What price honour? What price courage? What price love? There are some things which are beyond price and should not be bought or traded. To trade in honour or courage or love is to cheapen it.

❧

There is a special pleasure in doing what others have said cannot be done. Seek to prove them wrong by proving yourself to be right.

In every day, there is a moment of time in which a wish, fervently made, will be granted. But that moment is unknown. So, consider that every moment in every hour in every day is that moment, and wish fervently.

❁

Soiled goods are never a bargain.

❁

The best bargains are to be got from those in debt.

❁

Let the bargain suit the purpose.

It is possible to know the price of everything, and to know the value of nothing.

※

Speak first and soon surrender.

※

We are all wise, until we open our mouths and speak.

※

Looking is not seeing, listening is not hearing. Look and see. Listen and hear. Then act.

He that is ill to himself, will be ill to others.

✻

A man who loves not himself, loves no other.

✻

Remember that we all live in the shadow of others.

✻

A man who has no respect for himself, has no respect for others.

Ill-will never spoke well.

�֍

Ill-wishers are usually ill-doers.

✤

Many a friendship has been destroyed by envy. Envy cannot dwell in a noble soul.

✤

He that seeks trouble will usually find it. It would be good not to be with him when it arrives.

✤

A hasty man never wants for woe.

Lie down with dogs and rise up with fleas.

Wilful waste and woeful want: two halves of the same coin.

It is far easier to keep the devil out, than to turn him away.

Be aware that the devil often wears the face of an angel. But he will always speak with the tongue of the devil.

What the ear has not heard, the heart will not worry about.

❁

One should not get everything one wishes for; something should remain, so that there should always be something left to wish for. When there is nothing left to wish for, there is nothing left to live for.

❁

It is impossible to do good to others without also doing good for oneself.

❁

Reward is not always immediate. But it will come.

Think swiftly, speak softly, act wisely.

❧

Least said, and soonest mended.

❧

A hasty word, hastily spoken is as difficult to retrieve as a straw in the wind.

❧

A shout is often distorted, a whisper often unheard. The softest words are more easily listened to.

❧

Loud of voice – silent of deed.

The man who cannot speak, cannot listen,
The man who always speaks, never listens.

❧

An empty house is better than a difficult
tenant.

❧

Begin with a single handful. Soon you will
have the load.

❧

No one remembers when you are in the
right; everyone remembers when you are in
the wrong.

When you have put your hand into the dog's mouth, have a care to remove it carefully.

❧

Every patient becomes his own doctor — but only after he is cured.

❧

Clothes do not make the man, talk does not make the man. Only deeds make the man.

❧

The work is done and over. And when the tiredness leaves, the profit remains.

The proof of the pudding is in the eating.

✯

There is no satisfaction in a job half-done. Better undone than half-done.

✯

The work praises the man. Take pride in the work.

✯

To every cow its calf, to every book its copy. Every created thing is a reflection of its creator.

A heavy purse only indicates a heavy pocket and not a light heart.

❧

A closed hand gets a clenched fist. An open hand gets an open hand.

❧

Stretch out your hand in giving and you will never stretch it out in want.

❧

Stretch out your hand in friendship and it will never be empty.

Halving the potato is easy when there is love.

※

All things are easier with love.

※

To understand the creator, one must first understand created things.

※

Follow your heart. It is oft wiser than your head.

A house is not a home and a home is not a place. It is who you are.

※

A man will not be found where he lives, but rather where he loves.

※

A man may live upon little, but he cannot live upon nothing at all. And no man can live without dignity and pride.

※

There is a place for candlelight: true, it is difficult to read by, but it will also not allow you to see the dust upon the floor.

This is for you and yours
And for mine and ours.
And if mine and ours
Ever come across you and yours,
I pray that you and yours will do
As much for mine and ours
As mine and ours have done
For you and yours.

❦

Men are like bagpipes — no sound comes
from them until they're full.

❦

Happiness and contentment is the road we
travel, and not the destination.

One pair of shoes with good soles is better than two pairs of good uppers, and no soles ... especially in the rain.

✺

There is little point in carrying an umbrella if your shoes need soles.

✺

A trout in the pot and a bird in the hand are better than the salmon in the river and two birds in the bush.

✺

It is easier to cure the disease in its early stages. Be ever attentive, be ever vigilant.

May the road always rise to meet you
May the wind be always at your back
May the sun shine warm upon your
    face
May the rain fall soft upon your back
And until we meet again,
May the Good Lord hold you soft in
    the hollow of His hand.

✦

It is always better to thrive late, than never
do well.

✦

Postpone till morning,
Postpone forever.

The lazy young man and the poor old man; two sides of the same coin.

✿

Seek always, for by looking for one thing, you will surely find another. But never look and you will never find anything.

✿

Establish the name for rising early, then you may rest abed all day.

✿

The willing horse carries the heaviest burden. Take a care not to overload the willing horse.

It is better to strike slow and often, than once and hard; it is better to measure twice and cut once. Thus is the work halved. And it is no delay to sharpen the tool while working.

One look forward is better than two looks behind.

Eventually, even the smallest of thorns causes festering. Attend to the thorn.

Praise the ripe field and not the green corn.

Chickens should never be counted until they have hatched.

Don't fry the fish until they have been landed.

The water is never missed until the well runs dry.

All tides ebb, except the tide of grace.

All promises are debts.
All debts must be honoured.

⚜

Forgetting a debt does not pay it.

⚜

Be steadfast in time of turmoil,
Be valiant in the pursuit of truth,
Be cautious in time of trouble.

⚜

Be not greedy, but always generous
And if not generous in coin, then be
generous in spirit.

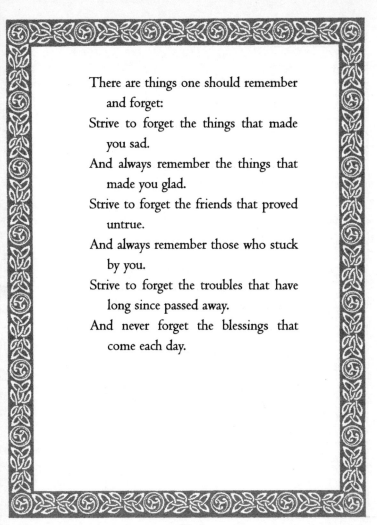

There are things one should remember
and forget:
Strive to forget the things that made
you sad.
And always remember the things that
made you glad.
Strive to forget the friends that proved
untrue.
And always remember those who stuck
by you.
Strive to forget the troubles that have
long since passed away.
And never forget the blessings that
come each day.

The victorious chieftain knows of his victory – before the battle has begun.

❁

A battle is won in the mind before it is fought in the field.

❁

When the chieftain falls, the battle fails.

❁

Faith lends substance. Belief is everything.

There is sometimes a bitterness in truth which makes it unpalatable.

❧

Necessity forges a plan and necessity knows no law.

❧

A nation without a language, is a nation without a soul. A man without honour is nothing.

❧

This is the truth of it: there are two sides to every story.

First the drink; then the story. Make sure to get the story first.

There is many a story in a glass of wine.

When the wine is inside, the sense is outside.

Nothing good was ever plotted at the bottom of a bottle.

Nothing empties a pocket quicker than wine.

❧

No matter how sweet the wine, there will always be a bitter reckoning in the morning.

❧

There is truth in wine. Listen to the truth. And it is only the sober who can hear the truth.

❧

There are many truths in wine, but they are often bitter truths.

He who comes with but a single story to tell will come away with two.

A good story is none the worse for being told twice.

Every tale grows in the telling; no story is ever shortened.

Leave the bad tale where you found it. It is not worthy of repeating.

At the heart of every legend there lies a grain of truth.

✻

Time is the greatest of storytellers.

✻

The traveller has tales to tell.
Every man should have tales to tell.
Every man should travel.

✻

Patience, like time, is a great healer. And where there is no cure, then patience is the greatest poultice.

With patience and time, a snail could crawl to Jerusalem.

※※

A good lock is a better safeguard than a suspicious mind.

※※

Patience is a virtue. There is no shame in virtue, no shame in patience.

※※

And, at the end, when all is said and done, all that remains is reputation. This endures. There is no finer legacy than an un-blemished reputation.

The wise man will leave something behind; a family, a home, a tree. And when all else has passed, the tree will remain. There is no finer tribute to a man.

❊

Far better the trouble that comes after death than the trouble that comes after shame.

❊

The ink of a scholar will survive longer than the blood of a martyr.

❊

For any achievement, the heart and the will must be ruled.

Accept each and every gift with the sure knowledge that most men give in the sure expectation of being paid – if not sooner, then certainly later.

※※※

No field is ever ploughed by being turned over in the mind.

※※※

May the face of good news, and the back of bad news be toward us. But if the news is ill, then let us face it. A thing quickly faced is soon dealt with and then forgotten.

This is my prayer:

  That there should be peace between
    neighbours,
  That there should be peace between kin
  That there should be peace between
    lovers
  That there should be peace within and
    without.

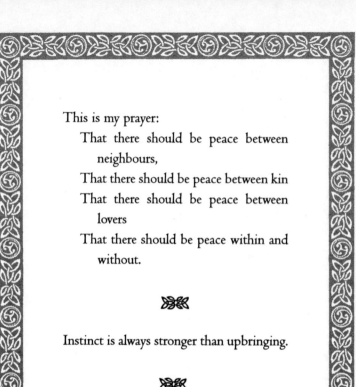

Instinct is always stronger than upbringing.

Sow in spring and reap in autumn; in life as in the seasons.

Happy the man who exists unknown to the law.

✺

Neither a law-breaker, nor a law-maker be. There is naught but unease in either occupation.

✺

The quietest piglet eats the most meal.

✺

The scarcer the fruit the sweeter it tastes.

Through stupidity and ill-chosen words, we often cut the stick with which we beat ourselves.

⁂

It is better to be rich in spirit than rich in wealth.

⁂

To keep loyalty in a man's heart, keep money in his purse.

⁂

A penny in your purse today is better than the promise of two pence tomorrow.

Food is a good workhorse. Hunger is good sauce.

❧

Far better to be in search of food, than to be in search of an appetite.

❧

The well-fed will never understand the hungry, unless they too have gone hungry.

❧

There is luck and there is discipline. Discipline achieves more.

You should be poor in misfortune,
You should be rich in blessings,
You should be slow to make enemies
And quick to make friends.

❧

God never closes one door, but that He opens another. Listen for the door opening and step through.

❧

Do not waste cherries on a pig or advice on a fool.

❧

Unasked for advice is never listened to.

It is the wise man who heeds the advice he would give to others.

❈

Two shorten the road.

❈

There is no heat, like the heat of shame,
There is no pain, like the pain of refusal,
There is no sorrow like the loss of a loved
one.

❈

There are some who have returned form
the mouth of the sea, but none that have
returned from the mouth of the grave.

This is my prayer for you:

I pray that there will always be work for your hands to do,

I pray that your purse will always hold a coin or two.

I pray that the sun will always shine on you

I pray that a friend will always be near to you,

I pray that God will fill your heart with gladness to cheer you.

And I pray that you will say this prayer for me.

The red sky at night is the shepherd's delight, but the crimson sky in the morning is the shepherds' warning.

❄❄❄

When the haystacks are tightly secured, then there is no need to fear the wind. Preparation and preparedness is everything.

❄❄❄

It is better to be clever than strong.

May the Lord grant you food and clothes
   aplenty,
A feather pillow for your head,
And may you be forty years in heaven
Before the devil even knows you're dead.

❦

A heart should always be big enough to
safely enfold all of one's friends and
family;

   A house should be too small to hold
them all.

You can dress a goat in silks and fine raiment, but it will always be a goat.

※

Take great care not to mistake the goat's beard for a stallion's tail.

※

You for me,
And I for thee, and for no one else,
Your face to mine,
And your head turned away from all
others.

Oh woman, loved by me
Give me your heart, your soul and your
    body
And I will give you mine.

❧

Love at first sight, often happens in
twilight.

❧

Fool me once – shame on you,
Fool me twice – shame on me.

There is little shame in stealing, cheating and fighting, provided that,

> When you steal, you steal the heart of your sweetheart,
>
> When you cheat, you will cheat death, and
>
> When you fight, you will fight for a worthy cause.

❊

Beauty makes no pot boil.

❊

What fills the eye with gladness, does the same for the heart.

It is truly said that love is blind to blemishes and faults. Happy are those who are in love.

❧

There is but one cure for love – and that is marriage.

❧

The longest day – no matter how long its length – will surely end. And tomorrow begins anew.

❧

This is my wish for you – that I may see you grey and combing the hair of your grandchildren.

May the Good Lord keep you in the palm of his Hand and may He never close His fist too tight about you.

❦

The roof above us should never fall in, And those below should never fall out.

❦

The pup is bold in the shelter of his own doorway.

❦

Warm words on a cold evening, a full moon on a dark night and may the road to your own door be downhill.

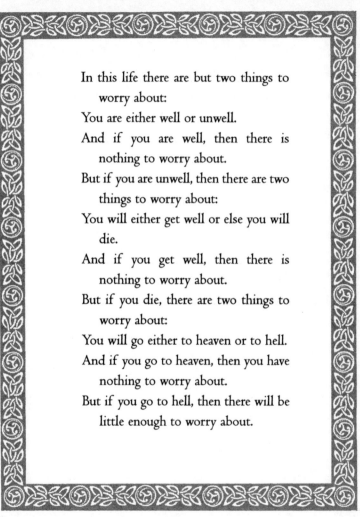

In this life there are but two things to
worry about:

You are either well or unwell.

And if you are well, then there is
nothing to worry about.

But if you are unwell, then there are two
things to worry about:

You will either get well or else you will
die.

And if you get well, then there is
nothing to worry about.

But if you die, there are two things to
worry about:

You will go either to heaven or to hell.

And if you go to heaven, then you have
nothing to worry about.

But if you go to hell, then there will be
little enough to worry about.

'What you and I accept as normal, everyday parts of life, our children's children will wonder at...'

Amergin to Eber Donn

'We honour the land which supports us, we respect the waters which give us life.'

Amergin the Bard

'We are the Three that is One and the One is the Land. We are the spirit of the place, the essence of the earth and the water, the forests, the lakes, the cliffs and the bogs. We are the Land.'

Banba, Fodla and Eriu

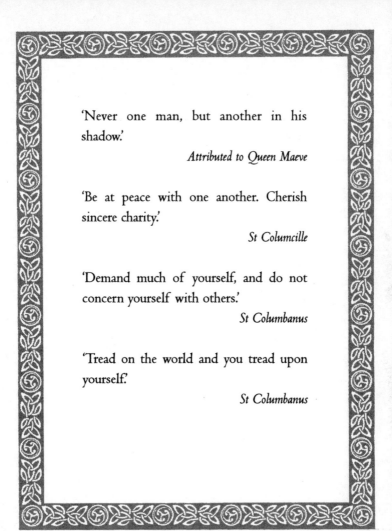

'Never one man, but another in his shadow.'

Attributed to Queen Maeve

'Be at peace with one another. Cherish sincere charity.'

St Columcille

'Demand much of yourself, and do not concern yourself with others.'

St Columbanus

'Tread on the world and you tread upon yourself.'

St Columbanus

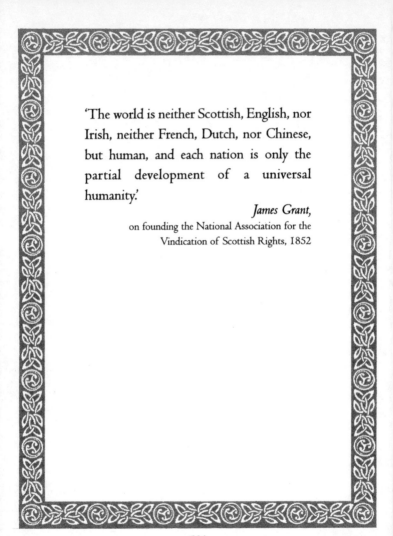

'The world is neither Scottish, English, nor Irish, neither French, Dutch, nor Chinese, but human, and each nation is only the partial development of a universal humanity.'

James Grant,
on founding the National Association for the
Vindication of Scottish Rights, 1852

WE SAW A VISION

The bardic tradition lives on.

Every age brings forth a new scholar, a new poet. It is fitting that the last piece in this collection was published as recently as 1976, and yet, the bards of a thousand years ago would surely have recognised it as being written by one of their own.

Knowledge grows in every age. We must grow with it and into it.

Rinneadh Aisling Dúinn ~
We Saw a Vision

In the darkness of despair, we saw a vision. We lit the light of hope. And it was not extinguished. In the desert of discouragement we saw a vision. We planted the tree of valour.

And it blossomed.

In the Winter of bondage, we saw a vision. We melted the snow of lethargy.

And the river of resurrection flowed from it.

We sent our vision aswim like a swan on the river. The vision became a reality. Winter became Summer. Bondage became Freedom.

And this we left to you as your inheritance.

Oh Generations of Freedom, remember us, the Generations of the Vision...

Liam MacUistin, 1976
Inscription on the wall of the National Garden of
Remembrance, Dublin, Ireland

THE CELTIC SPIRIT
Daily Meditations for the Turning Year

CAITLIN MATTHEWS

The ancient Celts and their spiritual mediators believed in the communion of all living things and sought harmony between nature and the human soul. With this inspiring book of day-by-day mediations, Celtic scholar Caitlin Matthews shows you how to reawaken the power of this age-old spiritual inheritance.

HODDER & STOUGHTON

THE ART OF HAPPINESS
A Handbook for Living

HH Dalai Lama and
Howard C Cutler

In this unique and important book, one of the world's great spiritual leaders offers his practical wisdom and advice on how we can overcome everyday human problems and achieve lasting happiness. For the many who wish to understand more about the Dalai Lama's approach to living, there has never been a book which brings his beliefs so vividly into the real world.

HODDER & STOUGHTON